A Kid's Guide to
INCREDIBLE TECHNOLOGY™

The Incredible Story of Computers and the Internet

Greg Roza

The Rosen Publishing Group's
PowerKids Press™
New York

For Shanna

Published in 2004 by The Rosen Publishing Group, Inc.
29 East 21st Street, New York, NY 10010

First Edition

Editor: Kathy Kuhtz Campbell
Book Design: Mike Donnellan

Photo Credits: p. 4 right by Mike Donnellan; p. 12 © Digital Art/CORBIS.
Illustrations by Leonello Calvetti.

Roza, Greg.
The incredible story of computers and the Internet / Greg Roza.
    v. cm.—(A kid's guide to incredible technology)
Includes bibliographical references and index.
Contents: The world of computers—What is a network?—A network of networks—What is a modem?—Faster is better—The World Wide Web—Just browsing—How does e-mail work?—What is a virus?—The Internet and beyond.
  ISBN 0-8239-6717-4 (library binding)
1. Internet—Juvenile literature. 2. Microcomputers—Juvenile literature. [1. Internet. 2. Microcomputers.] I. Title. II. Series.
  TK5105.875.I57 R74 2004
  004.67'8—dc21

                                                                    2002154261

Manufactured in the United States of America

Contents

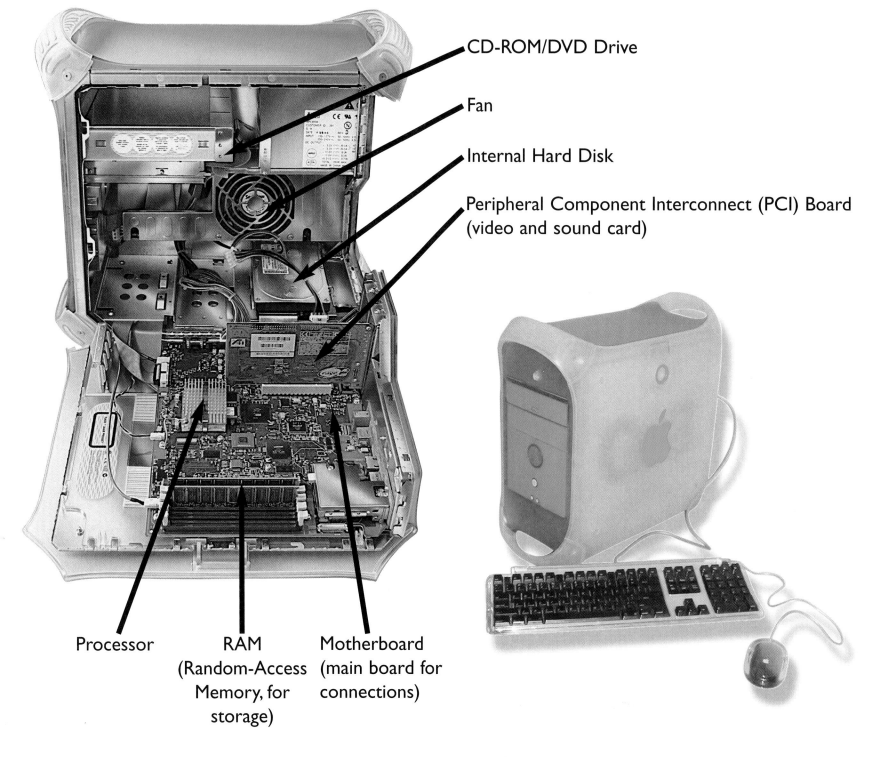

CD-ROM/DVD Drive

Fan

Internal Hard Disk

Peripheral Component Interconnect (PCI) Board
(video and sound card)

Processor

RAM
(Random-Access
Memory, for
storage)

Motherboard
(main board for
connections)

The World of Computers

Computers and computer **technology** affect our lives every day. For example, microwaves and TVs use computers to work. When we think about computers, we usually think of personal computers, or PCs. A PC is several machines that work together. Computer machinery, such as a keyboard, is called hardware. Computers also need **software** to work. The operating system is the most important software. It lets a computer's parts and **programs** work together, and lets users "talk" with the computers.

Computers **process information**, or data. Someone can enter the data by using a keyboard or a mouse. The data can come from a **CD-ROM** or from a computer that is on-line, meaning it is connected to the Internet. After a computer processes data, it shows the data on a display surface called a screen. It also stores the data on a **hard disk** or sends it to a computer that is on-line.

Left: Inside this computer is the "brain," or the Central Processing Unit (CPU). A CPU is called a microprocessor because it is very small. It is usually just called a processor.
Right: The same computer is shown closed, along with a keyboard and a mouse.

What Is a Network?

Two or more computers that are joined to share information are called a network. Networking lets one computer send data to and receive data from another computer. It also lets the computers use the same printer. A network of PCs that are joined by cables within a building, such as a business might have, is a Local Area Network (LAN). Most LANs are joined by an Ethernet network. It is called Ethernet because of the kind of technology and wiring that is used to connect computers to the network. Each of these computers has an Ethernet card, which is built into the computer. An Ethernet cable connects the computer to the network, where another computer, called a server, stores and shares data from all the computers that are joined to the network. A Wide Area Network (WAN) connects PCs that can be many miles (km) apart by using telephone or cable TV lines or **satellites**.

Top: Each computer in a LAN is usually joined by cable to a hub, a machine that contains many connections. Bottom: An Ethernet cable plugs into this special card for an Ethernet network connection. Networks can also be connected with telephone lines or power lines in a building.

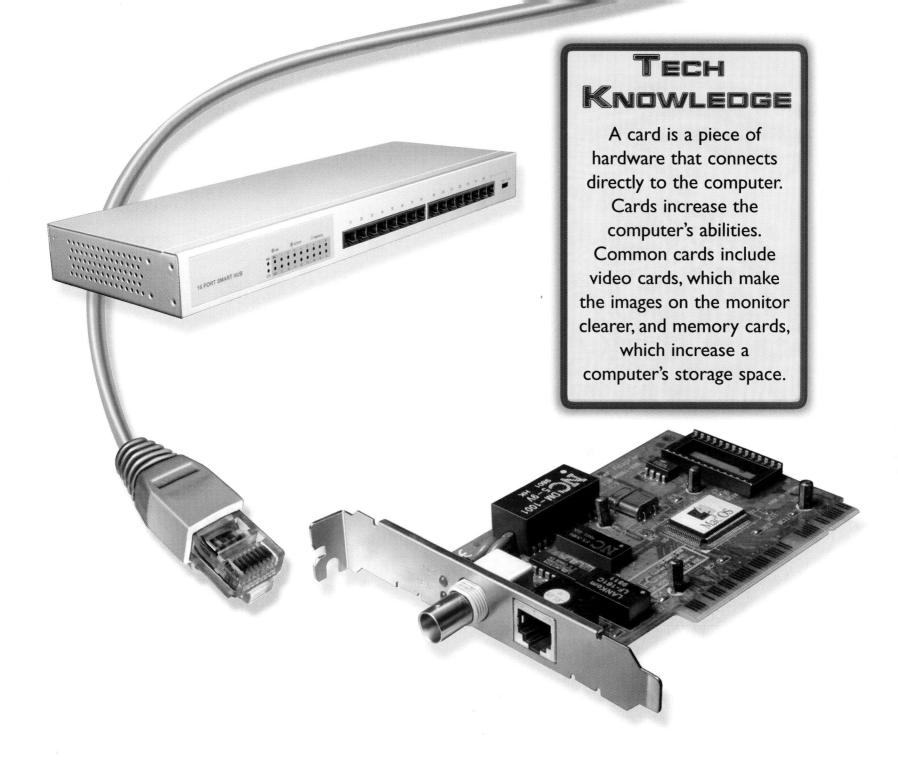

16 PORT SMART HUB

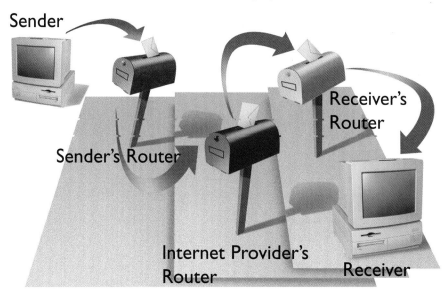

Internet Protocol (IP)

Sender

Sender's Router

Receiver's Router

Internet Provider's Router

Receiver

Transmission Control Protocol (TCP)

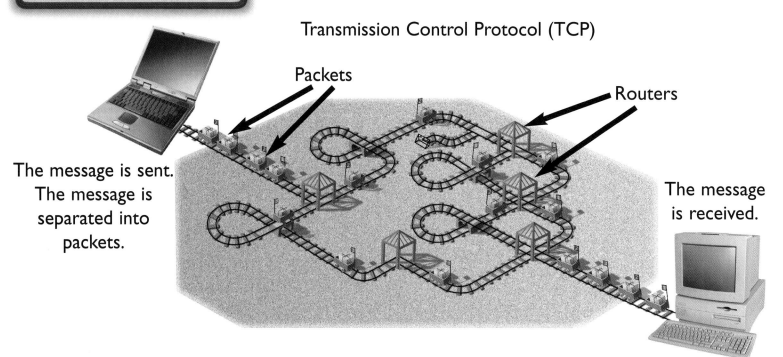

Packets

Routers

The message is sent. The message is separated into packets.

The message is received.

A Network of Networks

The Internet, or Net, is a worldwide network of networks. Computers that are connected to the Net can share information. Internet Service Providers, or ISPs, supply the use of the Net to a certain area of the world. Some ISPs own high-speed **fiber-optic** lines, undersea cables, and satellites, which form the "backbone" of the Net by joining ISPs worldwide. ISPs pay to use these lines to connect their users' computers to every computer on the Net.

For computers to speak with one another on the Internet, they use protocols, or special rules. The Net's two main protocols are the **Transmission** Control Protocol (TCP) and the Internet Protocol (IP). TCP sends data in pieces called packets and makes sure the packets are put together in the correct order. The IP labels each piece of data with a number that works like a post office address. The IP is responsible for moving the data to where it needs to go.

Top: When a computer's router sends data packets over the Net, it sends them to another router that is one step closer to the receiver's computer. The steps are repeated until the receiver's computer gets the data. Bottom: Data packets are sent on different paths, but all arrive at the receiver's computer, where they are put back together.

What Is a Modem?

A computer needs a modem to use the Internet. "Modem" is short for "modulator-demodulator." Something that is modulated is changed into a new form. A modem is a tool that is used with a computer to allow the computer's language to be changed into sounds and sent over phone lines. Phone lines carry these sounds as they carry people's voices. When the sounds reach the receiving modem, they are demodulated, or changed back into a form that a computer understands.

Another kind of modem called a digital subscriber line, or DSL, modem lets computers be always connected to the Net. It sends and receives data that is already in a language that a computer can understand. Though a DSL modem uses phone lines, it can send and receive data at higher speeds than a standard modem.

Cable modems use cable TV lines for a fast connection to the Net. Cable modems send Internet data to a PC over a cable TV line using the same amount of space that a cable TV channel uses on the line. Data sent from a PC back to the Net needs less space on the line because most users receive more data than they send.

Tech Knowledge

The language that computers understand is called binary code. Binary code is made up of electrical codes represented by two digits, 0 and 1, which a computer understands as "off" and "on." A single binary digit is called a bit, and 8 bits equal 1 byte. This system is called a digital system.

Modem

OH   SD   RD   TR

POWER

Bits and Bandwidth

Bandwidth is a measure of the amount of data that can pass through a connection at a given time. Bandwidth on a digital system, such as that on a computer, is measured in bits per second (bps). Modems joined to phone lines can send and receive up to 56,000 bps, or about 56 kilobits per second (Kbps). One kilobit equals 1,000 bits. Broadband, or high-speed, lines that use satellite-based service can send data at the same rate as phone lines but receive data at a much faster rate, about 400 Kbps. Modems that connect to cable TV lines send up to 10,000 Kbps and receive up to 30,000 Kbps. People using cable modems in an area share the bandwidth of one cable line, so the more users on-line at once, the slower a connection to send or receive data will be. Fiber-optic cables carry up to 10 gigabits per second (Gbps). One gigabit equals 1,000,000,000 bps.

Bottom: A coaxial cable is a type of wire that is used in cable TV lines and for computer networks connected to them. Top: Using glass threads to send data, fiber-optic cables can carry more data than coaxial cables or telephone lines.

The World Wide Web

The World Wide Web, or the Web, is the most popular part of the Internet. By using the Web, a person can find homework help, video games, library collections, and music. That person can even shop or pay bills on-line. The Web is based on a technology called **hypertext**. A **hyperlink**, or link, is a word, a phrase, or a picture on a Web page that takes you to another Web page when you use your mouse to click on it. This technology creates a "web" of connected pages and files.

The Web servers that store Web pages have their own IP address just as do all computers that are on-line. The numbers of an IP address tell where the server is and to which network it belongs. The numbers are given a name, called a domain name, so that users can remember them easily. It is much easier to recall www.powerkidspress.com than it is to recall 65.114.244.217.

Hypertext transfer protocol, or http, are rules that govern how Web pages, such as these, are carried between Web servers and computers. Http rules say that files or Web pages being sent over the Internet may include links to other files or pages. URLs that begin with "http://" tell the server to send the page to a computer using http.

TECH KNOWLEDGE

A uniform resource locator, or URL, is the address of a certain Web page or file on the Internet. The URL http://www.powerkidspress.com/download.html has three parts. The first part, http://, tells a computer what protocol is to be used. The second, www.powerkidspress.com, is the domain name of a Web server. The third part, download.html, shows a certain file that can be found on that Web page.

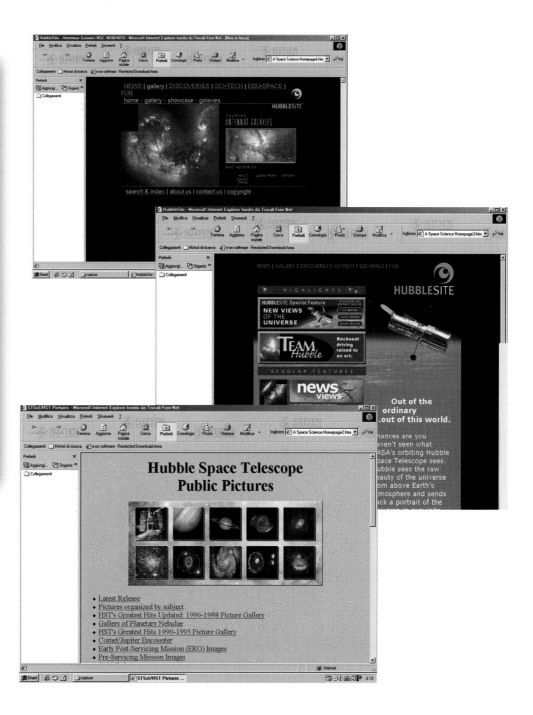

TECH KNOWLEDGE

HTML tags tell a Web browser how a Web page should look. HTML tags are often used in pairs. They have an opening tag and a closing tag. If a Web page designer wants a word to appear in heavy type, called boldface, the designer uses the opening tag <b> and the closing tag </b>, for example <b>word</b>.

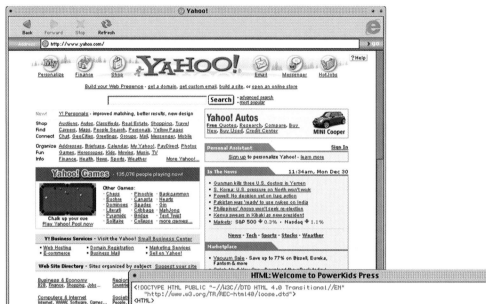

Just Browsing

A Web browser is software that lets the ISP's server know for which Web page you are looking. The software is used to locate and display Web pages. Internet Explorer and Netscape Navigator are two popular browsing programs. When you type a URL into a browser, the browser changes it into an IP address and then sends the request for that Web page to the ISP's server. The server locates the Web page and sends it to your browser.

After receiving the Web page, the browser displays it on your computer's screen. To display a page, a browser reads a language called Hypertext Markup Language, or HTML. This is the language that is used to write all Web pages and to set up links between Web pages. HTML is plain text, or words, with special "tags" that tell the browser how the Web page should look when it appears on your screen.

Top: *Search engines are programs that can be reached through a Web page on the Internet. Search engines, such as Yahoo!, help people to find information when words and phrases are typed into them.* Bottom and Left: *These pages show a page written in HTML and how that page looks on the display screen of a computer.*

How Does E-mail Work?

E-mail is short for electronic mail. Electronic means electric powered. E-mail is often thought of as a simple message sent quickly from one computer to another. E-mail is the electronic sending of messages, letters, and files between servers by using Simple Mail Transfer Protocol (SMTP). To get the messages from a server, an E-mail client uses Post Office Protocol (POP) or Internet Message Access Protocol (IMAP). An E-mail client is a program that allows you to create, send, and receive E-mail. When someone sends you E-mail, that person's E-mail client sends it to a POP server. When you check your E-mail, the POP server sends your messages to your E-mail client. Each ISP supplies E-mail addresses to users who join that ISP's network. Each address has a user name, the @, or "at" symbol, and the ISP's domain name. An example is yourname@yourISP.com.

An E-mail client, such as Microsoft Outlook Express, lets you create, send, receive, and organize E-mail. It also allows you to include an attachment, which is a file or a group of files, with your E-mail. Having the ability to send attachments lets you send important files, such as photos and sound files, to someone over the Internet.

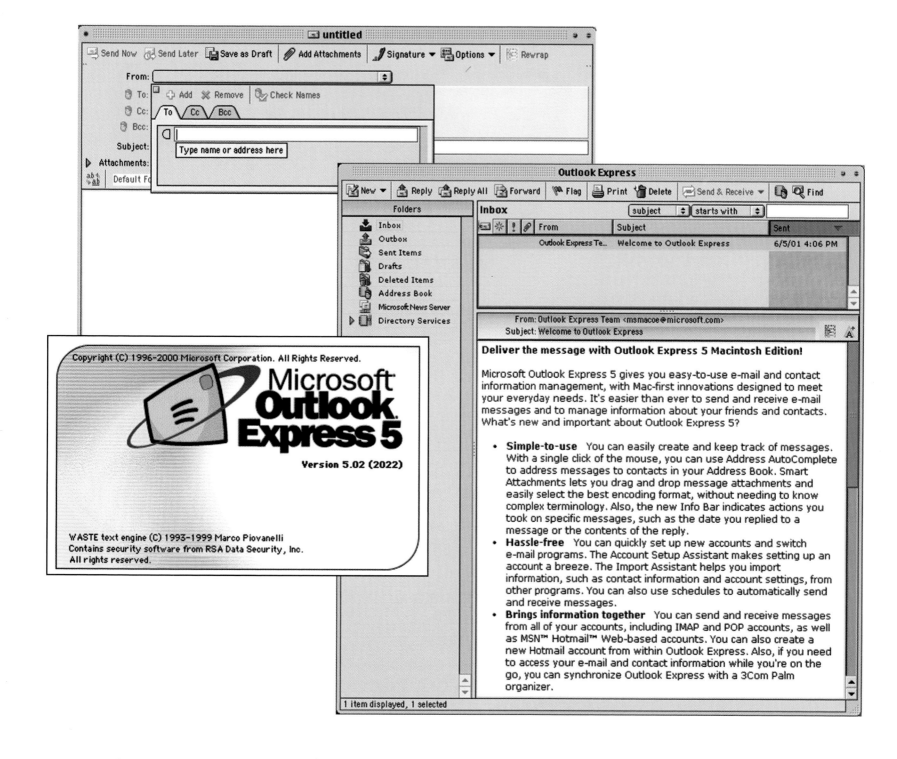

untitled

Send Now | Send Later | Save as Draft | Add Attachments | Signature ▼ | Options ▼ | Rewrap

From: [   ] ▼

To: | Add | ✖ Remove | Check Names

Cc: | To \ Cc \ Bcc

Bcc: | [   ]

Subject: | Type name or address here

Attachments:

ab↕ ↕ab Default Fo...

Outlook Express

New ▼ | Reply | Reply All | Forward | Flag | Print | Delete | Send & Receive ▼ | Find

Folders

- Inbox
- Outbox
- Sent Items
- Drafts
- Deleted Items
- Address Book
- Microsoft News Server
- Directory Services

Inbox | subject ⬍ starts with ⬍ [   ]

				From	Subject	Sent ▼
				Outlook Express Te...	Welcome to Outlook Express	6/5/01 4:06 PM

From: Outlook Express Team <msmacoe@microsoft.com>
Subject: Welcome to Outlook Express

Deliver the message with Outlook Express 5 Macintosh Edition!

Microsoft Outlook Express 5 gives you easy-to-use e-mail and contact information management, with Mac-first innovations designed to meet your everyday needs. It's easier than ever to send and receive e-mail messages and to manage information about your friends and contacts. What's new and important about Outlook Express 5?

- **Simple-to-use**   You can easily create and keep track of messages. With a single click of the mouse, you can use Address AutoComplete to address messages to contacts in your Address Book. Smart Attachments lets you drag and drop message attachments and easily select the best encoding format, without needing to know complex terminology. Also, the new Info Bar indicates actions you took on specific messages, such as the date you replied to a message or the contents of the reply.
- **Hassle-free**   You can quickly set up new accounts and switch e-mail programs. The Account Setup Assistant makes setting up an account a breeze. The Import Assistant helps you import information, such as contact information and account settings, from other programs. You can also use schedules to automatically send and receive messages.
- **Brings information together**   You can send and receive messages from all of your accounts, including IMAP and POP accounts, as well as MSN™ Hotmail™ Web-based accounts. You can also create a new Hotmail account from within Outlook Express. Also, if you need to access your e-mail and contact information while you're on the go, you can synchronize Outlook Express with a 3Com Palm organizer.

1 item displayed, 1 selected

TECH KNOWLEDGE

A firewall is a computer or a group of computers that is connected to a network or a PC and the Internet. By using both hardware and software, a firewall can study incoming packets of data. If the data follows certain protocols, the firewall allows the data to get through to the network or computer.

TIMELINE

1969 The U.S. military group Advanced Research Projects Agency (ARPA) develops the first long-distance computer network, ARPANET.

1971 The first E-mail program is created by American Ray Tomlinson.

1975 Satellites are used to link computer networks in the United States and Britain.

1984 The domain name system is introduced.

1989 Scientists in Geneva, Switzerland, begin using a new form of computer technology called Hypertext Markup Language, which was designed by Tim Berners-Lee.

1991 Tim Berners-Lee develops the World Wide Web using Hypertext Transfer Markup Language.

1998 The Internet Corporation for Assigned Names and Numbers is formed to oversee IP addresses and domain names on the Internet.

2002 The number of people in the world who are connected to the Internet reaches about 689,000,000.

Stay Safe on the Net

Some people use the Internet to cause problems for other computer users. They write a type of software program, called a **virus**, that attacks other computers each time the program is opened. E-mail viruses pass from computer to computer through E-mail messages. Viruses can change or erase files and can even erase data in the hard disk. Viruses can only affect software.

Most businesses that provide goods and services on the Net can be trusted to keep your personal information safe, but there is a risk in giving out the information on-line. Some people have ways of getting data such as credit card numbers from on-line businesses. They use the data to steal money from people. A way to protect yourself from this is to **encrypt** the data that you send over the Net. Encryption is a way of making data unreadable and sending it to a computer that can make it readable.

A computer user can block harmful material from certain sites or E-mail so that they cannot be displayed on a computer. This is done using a software tool called a filter. A filter can be used on a PC at home, at school, or on the ISP's computer.

21

The Internet and Beyond

Web planners are working on ways to improve the Web. Something called the Semantic Web will allow electronic machines, including PCs and handheld devices, such as Personal Digital Assistants (PDAs) and cellular phones, to work together. The Semantic Web may be able to turn down your stereo when you pick up the phone, or plan your vacation for you! Computers on the Semantic Web will be able to make better use of the Web than the computers we operate today.

The InterPlaNet (IPN) is a form of the Internet that will be able to connect networks on Earth with networks on spaceships and even on other planets! Scientists at the National Aeronautics and Space Administration (NASA), which is the U.S. government's space department, are now working to create a backbone for the IPN, which they hope will aid in studying planets beyond Earth.

Glossary

CD-ROM (see-dee-ROM) A compact disc that can be used with a computer.

encrypt (in-KRIPT) To change data from one form into another.

fiber-optic (FY-buh-rop-tik) Using fiber optics, which are the bundles of glass fibers that can send data as bursts of light.

hard disk (HARD DISK) A metal plate that stores all the data and commands on a computer. Also called a hard drive.

hyperlink (HY-per-link) A link that connects one Web page to another.

hypertext (HY-per-tekst) A system for writing and displaying words that can be linked to other pages.

information (in-fer-MAY-shun) Knowledge or facts, also called data.

process (PRAH-ses) To change something by using a special series of steps.

programs (PROH-gramz) Lists of directions and commands that when started causes a computer to act in a certain way.

satellites (SA-til-yts) Spacecraft that circle the Earth.

software (SOFT-wayr) A set of commands that tell a computer how to do a certain task. Software is often called a program.

technology (tek-NAH-luh-jee) The way that people do something using tools, and the tools that they use.

transmission (tranz-MIH-shun) The act of sending something from one place to another.

virus (VY-rus) A computer program that is designed to attack files or delete programs on other computers as soon as it is opened.

Index

B
bandwidth, 13
bits, 13

D
data, 5, 9, 13, 21
digital subscriber line (DSL),
10

E
E-mail, 18

F
fiber-optic cables, 13

H
Hypertext Markup Language
(HTML), 17

I
Internet, 9–10, 21
Internet Service Providers
(ISPs), 9, 18

M
modem(s), 10, 13

N
network(s), 6, 9, 14

P
PC(s), 5, 6, 22
protocols, 9, 18

S
satellites, 6
server(s), 14, 17–18
Simple Mail Transfer Protocol
(SMTP), 18

V
virus, 21

W
World Wide Web, 14, 17,
22

Web Sites

Due to the changing nature of Internet links, PowerKids Press has developed an on-line list of Web sites related to the subject of this book. This site is updated regularly. Please use this link to access the list:
www.powerkidslinks.com/kgit/computer/

24